ECCLESIASTES

BIBLE STUDY WORKBOOK

FULL TEXT OF ECCLESIASTES WITH
INDUCTIVE BIBLE STUDY QUESTIONS
& JOURNALING PAGES
World English Bible translation

How to Use This Workbook

Following each chapter are special sections to record your answers to the following study questions, with a few open prompts to get you thinking:

Who?
What?
Where?
When?
Why?
Wherefore? ("For what reason?")

These initial questions will encourage you to think deeply about all of the provided details in a given passage.

The next section is meant to help you interpret the passage correctly:

Content: *Instructions given, special or curious details provided, comparisons made, lists, questions and answers, figures of speech, etc.*

Context: *What is the context within the scripture? Read what happens in the passages before and after the one you're studying.*

Comparison: *A concordance is helpful here! Compare it to similar passages of scripture, to events or conversations that happen in a similar time or place, or to passages in other parts of the bible, both New and Old Testament.*

Culture: *Discover everything you can about what cultural influences may be present in the passage including the original language, references to historical figures, references to cultural practices or customs, etc.*

Consultation: *Look up **multiple** commentaries on the passage you're studying to discover what you may have missed.*

The version printed in this workbook is the WEB (World English Bible), a public domain translation.

For everything there is a season, and a time for every purpose under heaven

1 The words of the Preacher, the son of David, king in Jerusalem:

² "Vanity of vanities," says the Preacher; "Vanity of vanities, all is vanity." ³ What does man gain from all his labor in which he labors under the sun? ⁴ One generation goes, and another generation comes; but the earth remains forever. ⁵ The sun also rises, and the sun goes down, and hurries to its place where it rises. ⁶ The wind goes toward the south, and turns around to the north. It turns around continually as it goes, and the wind returns again to its courses. ⁷ All the rivers run into the sea, yet the sea is not full. To the place where the rivers flow, there they flow again. ⁸ All things are full of weariness beyond uttering. The eye is not satisfied with seeing, nor the ear filled with hearing. ⁹ That which has been is that which shall be; and that which has been done is that which shall be done: and there is no new thing under the sun. ¹⁰ Is there a thing of which it may be said, "Behold, this is new?" It has been long ago, in the ages which were before us. ¹¹ There is no memory of the former; neither shall there be any memory of the latter that are to come, among those that shall come after.

¹² I, the Preacher, was king over Israel in Jerusalem. ¹³ I applied my heart to seek and to search out by wisdom concerning all that is done under the sky. It is a heavy burden that God has given to the sons of men to be afflicted with. ¹⁴ I have seen all the works that are done under the sun; and behold, all is vanity and a chasing after wind. ¹⁵ That which is crooked can't be made straight; and that which is lacking can't be counted. ¹⁶ I said to myself, "Behold, I have obtained for myself great wisdom above all who were before me in Jerusalem. Yes, my heart has had great experience of wisdom and knowledge."

[17] I applied my heart to know wisdom, and to know madness and folly. I perceived that this also was a chasing after wind. [18] For in much wisdom is much grief; and he who increases knowledge increases sorrow.

OBSERVATION:
What do you notice? Write your questions.

WHO? Who speaks or is spoken to? Who is present or mentioned?

_____
_____
_____
_____
_____
_____

WHAT? What action or dialogue has taken place? What questions does this bring up?

_____
_____
_____
_____
_____
_____
_____
_____

WHERE? Whose house? What city? What nation?

_____
_____
_____
_____
_____
_____

WHEN? What time, what day, what week, after what, etc?

_____
_____
_____
_____
_____
_____

WHY? What led to the action or dialogue that took place in this passage? Record every question you have about the purpose for what is said or done.

_____
_____
_____
_____
_____
_____
_____
_____
_____
_____
_____

OTHER QUESTIONS & OBSERVATIONS

_____
_____
_____
_____
_____
_____
_____
_____
_____
_____
_____
_____

CONTENT Record figures of speech, questions and answers, lists, comparisons, etc. What questions do these bring up?

_____
_____
_____
_____
_____
_____
_____
_____
_____
_____

CONTEXT What is the immediate context and the broader context? What happens right before and after this passage?

_____
_____
_____
_____
_____
_____

COMPARISON Track down scripture quotations, compare similar passages, notice other uses in scripture of special terms, names, or ideas.

_____
_____
_____
_____
_____
_____
_____

CULTURE How does the cultural context influence this passage? What questions do you need answered about the culture to understand it better?

_____
_____
_____
_____
_____
_____
_____
_____
_____
_____

CONSULTATION Explore commentaries and sermons on this passage and record helpful thoughts.

_____
_____
_____
_____
_____
_____
_____
_____
_____
_____
_____
_____
_____

APPLICATION
Keeping in mind the meaning of this passage in its original context, how can you apply this passage to your life?

_____
_____
_____
_____
_____
_____
_____
_____
_____
_____
_____
_____
_____
_____
_____
_____
_____
_____
_____
_____
_____
_____
_____
_____
_____
_____
_____

2 I said in my heart, "Come now, I will test you with mirth: therefore enjoy pleasure;" and behold, this also was vanity. ² I said of laughter, "It is foolishness;" and of mirth, "What does it accomplish?"

³ I searched in my heart how to cheer my flesh with wine, my heart yet guiding me with wisdom, and how to lay hold of folly, until I might see what it was good for the sons of men that they should do under heaven all the days of their lives. ⁴ I made myself great works. I built myself houses. I planted myself vineyards. ⁵ I made myself gardens and parks, and I planted trees in them of all kinds of fruit. ⁶ I made myself pools of water, to water the forest where trees were grown. ⁷ I bought male servants and female servants, and had servants born in my house. I also had great possessions of herds and flocks, above all who were before me in Jerusalem. ⁸ I also gathered silver and gold for myself, and the treasure of kings and of the provinces. I got myself male and female singers, and the delights of the sons of men: musical instruments, and that of all sorts. ⁹ So I was great, and increased more than all who were before me in Jerusalem. My wisdom also remained with me. ¹⁰ Whatever my eyes desired, I didn't keep from them. I didn't withhold my heart from any joy, for my heart rejoiced because of all my labor, and this was my portion from all my labor. ¹¹ Then I looked at all the works that my hands had worked, and at the labor that I had labored to do; and behold, all was vanity and a chasing after wind, and there was no profit under the sun.

¹² I turned myself to consider wisdom, madness, and folly; for what can the king's successor do? Just that which has been done long ago. ¹³ Then I saw that wisdom excels folly, as far as light excels darkness.

14 The wise man's eyes are in his head, and the fool walks in darkness—and yet I perceived that one event happens to them all. **15** Then I said in my heart, "As it happens to the fool, so will it happen even to me; and why was I then more wise?" Then I said in my heart that this also is vanity. **16** For of the wise man, even as of the fool, there is no memory forever, since in the days to come all will have been long forgotten. Indeed, the wise man must die just like the fool!

17 So I hated life, because the work that is worked under the sun was grievous to me; for all is vanity and a chasing after wind. **18** I hated all my labor in which I labored under the sun, because I must leave it to the man who comes after me. **19** Who knows whether he will be a wise man or a fool? Yet he will have rule over all of my labor in which I have labored, and in which I have shown myself wise under the sun. This also is vanity.

20 Therefore I began to cause my heart to despair concerning all the labor in which I had labored under the sun. **21** For there is a man whose labor is with wisdom, with knowledge, and with skillfulness; yet he shall leave it for his portion to a man who has not labored for it. This also is vanity and a great evil. **22** For what does a man have of all his labor and of the striving of his heart, in which he labors under the sun? **23** For all his days are sorrows, and his travail is grief; yes, even in the night his heart takes no rest. This also is vanity. **24** There is nothing better for a man than that he should eat and drink, and make his soul enjoy good in his labor. This also I saw, that it is from the hand of God. **25** For who can eat, or who can have enjoyment, more than I? **26** For to the man who pleases him, God gives wisdom, knowledge, and joy; but to the sinner he gives travail, to gather and to heap up, that he may give to him who pleases God. This also is vanity and a chasing after wind.

OBSERVATION:
What do you notice? Write your questions.

WHO?
Who speaks or is spoken to? Who is present or mentioned?

_____
_____
_____
_____
_____

WHAT?
What action or dialogue has taken place? What questions does this bring up?

_____
_____
_____
_____
_____
_____
_____

WHERE?
Whose house? What city? What nation?

_____
_____
_____
_____
_____

WHEN?
What time, what day, what week, after what, etc?

_____
_____
_____
_____
_____

WHY? What led to the action or dialogue that took place in this passage? Record every question you have about the purpose for what is said or done.

_____
_____
_____
_____
_____
_____
_____
_____
_____
_____

OTHER QUESTIONS & OBSERVATIONS

_____
_____
_____
_____
_____
_____
_____
_____
_____
_____
_____
_____
_____

CONTENT Record figures of speech, questions and answers, lists, comparisons, etc. What questions do these bring up?

_____
_____
_____
_____
_____
_____
_____
_____
_____
_____

CONTEXT What is the immediate context and the broader context? What happens right before and after this passage?

_____
_____
_____
_____
_____
_____

COMPARISON Track down scripture quotations, compare similar passages, notice other uses in scripture of special terms, names, or ideas.

_____
_____
_____
_____
_____
_____
_____

CULTURE
How does the cultural context influence this passage? What questions do you need answered about the culture to understand it better?

_____
_____
_____
_____
_____
_____
_____
_____
_____

CONSULTATION
Explore commentaries and sermons on this passage and record helpful thoughts.

_____
_____
_____
_____
_____
_____
_____
_____
_____
_____
_____
_____

APPLICATION
Keeping in mind the meaning of this passage in its original context, how can you apply this passage to your life?

_____
_____
_____
_____
_____
_____
_____
_____
_____
_____
_____
_____
_____
_____
_____
_____
_____
_____
_____
_____
_____
_____
_____
_____

3 For everything there is a season, and a time for every purpose under heaven:
² a time to be born, and a time to die;
a time to plant, and a time to pluck up that which is planted;
³ a time to kill, and a time to heal;
a time to break down, and a time to build up;
⁴ a time to weep, and a time to laugh;
a time to mourn, and a time to dance;
⁵ a time to cast away stones, and a time to gather stones together;
a time to embrace, and a time to refrain from embracing;
⁶ a time to seek, and a time to lose;
a time to keep, and a time to cast away;
⁷ a time to tear, and a time to sew;
a time to keep silence, and a time to speak;
⁸ a time to love, and a time to hate;
a time for war, and a time for peace.
⁹ What profit has he who works in that in which he labors? ¹⁰ I have seen the burden which God has given to the sons of men to be afflicted with. ¹¹ He has made everything beautiful in its time. He has also set eternity in their hearts, yet so that man can't find out the work that God has done from the beginning even to the end. ¹² I know that there is nothing better for them than to rejoice, and to do good as long as they live. ¹³ Also that every man should eat and drink, and enjoy good in all his labor, is the gift of God. ¹⁴ I know that whatever God does, it shall be forever. Nothing can be added to it, nor anything taken from it; and God has done it, that men should fear before him. ¹⁵ That which is has been long ago, and that which is to be has been long ago. God seeks again that which is passed away.

16 Moreover I saw under the sun, in the place of justice, that wickedness was there; and in the place of righteousness, that wickedness was there. **17** I said in my heart, "God will judge the righteous and the wicked; for there is a time there for every purpose and for every work." **18** I said in my heart, "As for the sons of men, God tests them, so that they may see that they themselves are like animals. **19** For that which happens to the sons of men happens to animals. Even one thing happens to them. As the one dies, so the other dies. Yes, they have all one breath; and man has no advantage over the animals; for all is vanity. **20** All go to one place. All are from the dust, and all turn to dust again. **21** Who knows the spirit of man, whether it goes upward, and the spirit of the animal, whether it goes downward to the earth?"

22 Therefore I saw that there is nothing better than that a man should rejoice in his works; for that is his portion: for who can bring him to see what will be after him?

OBSERVATION:

What do you notice? Write your questions.

WHO?
Who speaks or is spoken to? Who is present or mentioned?

_____

_____

_____

_____

_____

_____

WHAT?
What action or dialogue has taken place? What questions does this bring up?

_____

_____

_____

_____

_____

_____

_____

_____

WHERE?
Whose house? What city? What nation?

_____

_____

_____

_____

_____

WHEN?
What time, what day, what week, after what, etc?

_____

_____

_____

_____

_____

WHY? What led to the action or dialogue that took place in this passage? Record every question you have about the purpose for what is said or done.

_____
_____
_____
_____
_____
_____
_____
_____
_____
_____
_____
_____

OTHER QUESTIONS & OBSERVATIONS

_____
_____
_____
_____
_____
_____
_____
_____
_____
_____
_____
_____
_____
_____
_____
_____

CONTENT Record figures of speech, questions and answers, lists, comparisons, etc. What questions do these bring up?

_____
_____
_____
_____
_____
_____
_____
_____
_____

CONTEXT What is the immediate context and the broader context? What happens right before and after this passage?

_____
_____
_____
_____
_____
_____

COMPARISON Track down scripture quotations, compare similar passages, notice other uses in scripture of special terms, names, or ideas.

_____
_____
_____
_____
_____
_____

CULTURE How does the cultural context influence this passage? What questions do you need answered about the culture to understand it better?

_____
_____
_____
_____
_____
_____
_____
_____
_____

CONSULTATION Explore commentaries and sermons on this passage and record helpful thoughts.

_____
_____
_____
_____
_____
_____
_____
_____
_____
_____
_____
_____
_____

APPLICATION
Keeping in mind the meaning of this passage in its original context, how can you apply this passage to your life?

_____
_____
_____
_____
_____
_____
_____
_____
_____
_____
_____
_____
_____
_____
_____
_____
_____
_____
_____
_____
_____
_____
_____
_____
_____

4 Then I returned and saw all the oppressions that are done under the sun: and behold, the tears of those who were oppressed, and they had no comforter; and on the side of their oppressors there was power; but they had no comforter. **2** Therefore I praised the dead who have been long dead more than the living who are yet alive. **3** Yes, better than them both is him who has not yet been, who has not seen the evil work that is done under the sun. **4** Then I saw all the labor and achievement that is the envy of a man's neighbor. This also is vanity and a striving after wind. **5** The fool folds his hands together and ruins himself. **6** Better is a handful, with quietness, than two handfuls with labor and chasing after wind. **7** Then I returned and saw vanity under the sun. **8** There is one who is alone, and he has neither son nor brother. There is no end to all of his labor, neither are his eyes satisfied with wealth. "For whom then, do I labor and deprive my soul of enjoyment?" This also is vanity. Yes, it is a miserable business. **9** Two are better than one, because they have a good reward for their labor. **10** For if they fall, the one will lift up his fellow; but woe to him who is alone when he falls, and doesn't have another to lift him up. **11** Again, if two lie together, then they have warmth; but how can one keep warm alone? **12** If a man prevails against one who is alone, two shall withstand him; and a threefold cord is not quickly broken. **13** Better is a poor and wise youth than an old and foolish king who doesn't know how to receive admonition any more. **14** For out of prison he came out to be king; yes, even in his kingdom he was born poor. **15** I saw all the living who walk under the sun, that they were with the youth, the other, who succeeded him. **16** There was no end of all the people, even of all them over whom he was—yet those who come after shall not rejoice in him. Surely this also is vanity and a chasing after wind.

OBSERVATION:
What do you notice? Write your questions.

WHO? Who speaks or is spoken to? Who is present or mentioned?

_____

_____

_____

_____

_____

WHAT? What action or dialogue has taken place? What questions does this bring up?

_____

_____

_____

_____

_____

_____

WHERE? Whose house? What city? What nation?

_____

_____

_____

_____

WHEN? What time, what day, what week, after what, etc?

_____

_____

_____

_____

WHY? What led to the action or dialogue that took place in this passage? Record every question you have about the purpose for what is said or done.

_____
_____
_____
_____
_____
_____
_____
_____
_____
_____
_____

OTHER QUESTIONS & OBSERVATIONS

_____
_____
_____
_____
_____
_____
_____
_____
_____
_____
_____
_____
_____
_____
_____

CONTENT Record figures of speech, questions and answers, lists, comparisons, etc. What questions do these bring up?

_____
_____
_____
_____
_____
_____
_____
_____
_____
_____

CONTEXT What is the immediate context and the broader context? What happens right before and after this passage?

_____
_____
_____
_____
_____
_____
_____

COMPARISON Track down scripture quotations, compare similar passages, notice other uses in scripture of special terms, names, or ideas.

_____
_____
_____
_____
_____
_____
_____
_____

CULTURE
How does the cultural context influence this passage? What questions do you need answered about the culture to understand it better?

_____
_____
_____
_____
_____
_____
_____
_____
_____

CONSULTATION
Explore commentaries and sermons on this passage and record helpful thoughts.

_____
_____
_____
_____
_____
_____
_____
_____
_____
_____
_____
_____
_____
_____

APPLICATION
Keeping in mind the meaning of this passage in its original context, how can you apply this passage to your life?

_____
_____
_____
_____
_____
_____
_____
_____
_____
_____
_____
_____
_____
_____
_____
_____
_____
_____
_____
_____
_____
_____
_____
_____
_____

5 Guard your steps when you go to God's house; for to draw near to listen is better than to give the sacrifice of fools, for they don't know that they do evil. **2** Don't be rash with your mouth, and don't let your heart be hasty to utter anything before God; for God is in heaven, and you on earth. Therefore let your words be few. **3** For as a dream comes with a multitude of cares, so a fool's speech with a multitude of words. **4** When you vow a vow to God, don't defer to pay it; for he has no pleasure in fools. Pay that which you vow. **5** It is better that you should not vow, than that you should vow and not pay. **6** Don't allow your mouth to lead you into sin. Don't protest before the messenger that this was a mistake. Why should God be angry at your voice, and destroy the work of your hands? **7** For in the multitude of dreams there are vanities, as well as in many words; but you must fear God.

8 If you see the oppression of the poor, and the violent taking away of justice and righteousness in a district, don't marvel at the matter, for one official is eyed by a higher one, and there are officials over them. **9** Moreover the profit of the earth is for all. The king profits from the field.

10 He who loves silver shall not be satisfied with silver; nor he who loves abundance, with increase: this also is vanity. **11** When goods increase, those who eat them are increased; and what advantage is there to its owner, except to feast on them with his eyes?

12 The sleep of a laboring man is sweet, whether he eats little or much; but the abundance of the rich will not allow him to sleep.

13 There is a grievous evil which I have seen under the sun: wealth kept by its owner to his harm.

14 Those riches perish by misfortune, and if he has fathered a son, there is nothing in his hand. **15** As he came out of his mother's womb, naked shall he go again as he came, and shall take nothing for his labor, which he may carry away in his hand. **16** This also is a grievous evil, that in all points as he came, so shall he go. And what profit does he have who labors for the wind? **17** All his days he also eats in darkness, he is frustrated, and has sickness and wrath.

18 Behold, that which I have seen to be good and proper is for one to eat and to drink, and to enjoy good in all his labor, in which he labors under the sun, all the days of his life which God has given him; for this is his portion. **19** Every man also to whom God has given riches and wealth, and has given him power to eat of it, and to take his portion, and to rejoice in his labor—this is the gift of God. **20** For he shall not often reflect on the days of his life; because God occupies him with the joy of his heart.

OBSERVATION:
What do you notice? Write your questions.

WHO?
Who speaks or is spoken to? Who is present or mentioned?

_____
_____
_____
_____
_____
_____

WHAT?
What action or dialogue has taken place? What questions does this bring up?

_____
_____
_____
_____
_____
_____
_____

WHERE?
Whose house? What city? What nation?

_____
_____
_____
_____
_____

WHEN?
What time, what day, what week, after what, etc?

_____
_____
_____
_____
_____

WHY? What led to the action or dialogue that took place in this passage? Record every question you have about the purpose for what is said or done.

_____
_____
_____
_____
_____
_____
_____
_____
_____
_____
_____

OTHER QUESTIONS & OBSERVATIONS

_____
_____
_____
_____
_____
_____
_____
_____
_____
_____
_____
_____
_____

CONTENT
Record figures of speech, questions and answers, lists, comparisons, etc. What questions do these bring up?

_____
_____
_____
_____
_____
_____
_____
_____
_____

CONTEXT
What is the immediate context and the broader context? What happens right before and after this passage?

_____
_____
_____
_____
_____
_____

COMPARISON
Track down scripture quotations, compare similar passages, notice other uses in scripture of special terms, names, or ideas.

_____
_____
_____
_____
_____
_____

CULTURE
How does the cultural context influence this passage? What questions do you need answered about the culture to understand it better?

_____

_____

_____

_____

_____

_____

_____

_____

_____

_____

CONSULTATION
Explore commentaries and sermons on this passage and record helpful thoughts.

_____

_____

_____

_____

_____

_____

_____

_____

_____

_____

_____

_____

_____

_____

APPLICATION
Keeping in mind the meaning of this passage in its original context, how can you apply this passage to your life?

_____

_____

_____

_____

_____

_____

_____

_____

_____

_____

_____

_____

_____

_____

_____

_____

_____

_____

_____

_____

_____

_____

_____

_____

_____

_____

6 There is an evil which I have seen under the sun, and it is heavy on men: **2** a man to whom God gives riches, wealth, and honor, so that he lacks nothing for his soul of all that he desires, yet God gives him no power to eat of it, but an alien eats it. This is vanity, and it is an evil disease.

3 If a man fathers a hundred children, and lives many years, so that the days of his years are many, but his soul is not filled with good, and moreover he has no burial; I say that a stillborn child is better than he: **4** for it comes in vanity, and departs in darkness, and its name is covered with darkness. **5** Moreover it has not seen the sun nor known it. This has rest rather than the other. **6** Yes, though he live a thousand years twice told, and yet fails to enjoy good, don't all go to one place? **7** All the labor of man is for his mouth, and yet the appetite is not filled. **8** For what advantage has the wise more than the fool? What has the poor man, that knows how to walk before the living? **9** Better is the sight of the eyes than the wandering of the desire. This also is vanity and a chasing after wind. **10** Whatever has been, its name was given long ago; and it is known what man is; neither can he contend with him who is mightier than he. **11** For there are many words that create vanity. What does that profit man? **12** For who knows what is good for man in life, all the days of his vain life which he spends like a shadow? For who can tell a man what will be after him under the sun?

OBSERVATION:

What do you notice? Write your questions.

WHO? Who speaks or is spoken to? Who is present or mentioned?

_____
_____
_____
_____
_____
_____

WHAT? What action or dialogue has taken place? What questions does this bring up?

_____
_____
_____
_____
_____
_____
_____

WHERE? Whose house? What city? What nation?

_____
_____
_____
_____
_____

WHEN? What time, what day, what week, after what, etc?

_____
_____
_____
_____
_____

WHY? What led to the action or dialogue that took place in this passage? Record every question you have about the purpose for what is said or done.

_____
_____
_____
_____
_____
_____
_____
_____
_____
_____

OTHER QUESTIONS & OBSERVATIONS

_____
_____
_____
_____
_____
_____
_____
_____
_____
_____
_____
_____
_____

CONTENT Record figures of speech, questions and answers, lists, comparisons, etc. What questions do these bring up?

_____
_____
_____
_____
_____
_____
_____
_____
_____
_____

CONTEXT What is the immediate context and the broader context? What happens right before and after this passage?

_____
_____
_____
_____
_____

COMPARISON Track down scripture quotations, compare similar passages, notice other uses in scripture of special terms, names, or ideas.

_____
_____
_____
_____
_____
_____

CULTURE
How does the cultural context influence this passage? What questions do you need answered about the culture to understand it better?

_____
_____
_____
_____
_____
_____
_____
_____
_____

CONSULTATION
Explore commentaries and sermons on this passage and record helpful thoughts.

_____
_____
_____
_____
_____
_____
_____
_____
_____
_____
_____
_____
_____

APPLICATION
Keeping in mind the meaning of this passage in its original context, how can you apply this passage to your life?

_____

_____

_____

_____

_____

_____

_____

_____

_____

_____

_____

_____

_____

_____

_____

_____

_____

_____

_____

_____

_____

_____

_____

_____

_____

_____

7 A good name is better than fine perfume; and the day of death better than the day of one's birth. **2** It is better to go to the house of mourning than to go to the house of feasting; for that is the end of all men, and the living should take this to heart. **3** Sorrow is better than laughter; for by the sadness of the face the heart is made good. **4** The heart of the wise is in the house of mourning; but the heart of fools is in the house of mirth. **5** It is better to hear the rebuke of the wise than for a man to hear the song of fools. **6** For as the crackling of thorns under a pot, so is the laughter of the fool. This also is vanity. **7** Surely extortion makes the wise man foolish; and a bribe destroys the understanding. **8** Better is the end of a thing than its beginning. The patient in spirit is better than the proud in spirit. **9** Don't be hasty in your spirit to be angry, for anger rests in the bosom of fools. **10** Don't say, "Why were the former days better than these?" For you do not ask wisely about this.

11 Wisdom is as good as an inheritance. Yes, it is more excellent for those who see the sun. **12** For wisdom is a defense, even as money is a defense; but the excellency of knowledge is that wisdom preserves the life of him who has it.

13 Consider the work of God, for who can make that straight, which he has made crooked? **14** In the day of prosperity be joyful, and in the day of adversity consider; yes, God has made the one side by side with the other, to the end that man should not find out anything after him.

15 All this I have seen in my days of vanity: there is a righteous man who perishes in his righteousness, and there is a wicked man who lives long in his evildoing. **16** Don't be overly righteous, neither make yourself overly wise. Why should you destroy yourself?

17 Don't be too wicked, neither be foolish. Why should you die before your time? **18** It is good that you should take hold of this. Yes, also don't withdraw your hand from that; for he who fears God will come out of them all. **19** Wisdom is a strength to the wise man more than ten rulers who are in a city. **20** Surely there is not a righteous man on earth who does good and doesn't sin. **21** Also don't take heed to all words that are spoken, lest you hear your servant curse you; **22** for often your own heart knows that you yourself have likewise cursed others. **23** All this I have proved in wisdom. I said, "I will be wise;" but it was far from me. **24** That which is, is far off and exceedingly deep. Who can find it out? **25** I turned around, and my heart sought to know and to search out, and to seek wisdom and the scheme of things, and to know that wickedness is stupidity, and that foolishness is madness. **26** I find more bitter than death the woman whose heart is snares and traps, whose hands are chains. Whoever pleases God shall escape from her; but the sinner will be ensnared by her. **27** "Behold, I have found this," says the Preacher, "to one another, to find out the scheme **28** which my soul still seeks, but I have not found. I have found one man among a thousand, but I have not found a woman among all those. **29** Behold, I have only found this: that God made man upright; but they search for many schemes."

OBSERVATION:
What do you notice? Write your questions.

WHO? Who speaks or is spoken to? Who is present or mentioned?

_____
_____
_____
_____
_____

WHAT? What action or dialogue has taken place? What questions does this bring up?

_____
_____
_____
_____
_____
_____
_____

WHERE? Whose house? What city? What nation?

_____
_____
_____
_____
_____
_____

WHEN? What time, what day, what week, after what, etc?

_____
_____
_____
_____
_____
_____

WHY? What led to the action or dialogue that took place in this passage? Record every question you have about the purpose for what is said or done.

_____
_____
_____
_____
_____
_____
_____
_____
_____
_____
_____

OTHER QUESTIONS & OBSERVATIONS

_____
_____
_____
_____
_____
_____
_____
_____
_____
_____
_____
_____
_____
_____
_____
_____
_____

CONTENT
Record figures of speech, questions and answers, lists, comparisons, etc. What questions do these bring up?

_____
_____
_____
_____
_____
_____
_____
_____
_____
_____

CONTEXT
What is the immediate context and the broader context? What happens right before and after this passage?

_____
_____
_____
_____
_____
_____
_____

COMPARISON
Track down scripture quotations, compare similar passages, notice other uses in scripture of special terms, names, or ideas.

_____
_____
_____
_____
_____
_____
_____
_____

CULTURE How does the cultural context influence this passage? What questions do you need answered about the culture to understand it better?

_____
_____
_____
_____
_____
_____
_____
_____

CONSULTATION Explore commentaries and sermons on this passage and record helpful thoughts.

_____
_____
_____
_____
_____
_____
_____
_____
_____
_____
_____
_____
_____

APPLICATION
Keeping in mind the meaning of this passage in its original context, how can you apply this passage to your life?

_____
_____
_____
_____
_____
_____
_____
_____
_____
_____
_____
_____
_____
_____
_____
_____
_____
_____
_____
_____
_____
_____
_____
_____
_____
_____

8 Who is like the wise man? And who knows the interpretation of a thing? A man's wisdom makes his face shine, and the hardness of his face is changed. **2** I say, "Keep the king's command!" because of the oath to God. **3** Don't be hasty to go out of his presence. Don't persist in an evil thing, for he does whatever pleases him, **4** for the king's word is supreme. Who can say to him, "What are you doing?" **5** Whoever keeps the commandment shall not come to harm, and his wise heart will know the time and procedure. **6** For there is a time and procedure for every purpose, although the misery of man is heavy on him. **7** For he doesn't know that which will be; for who can tell him how it will be? **8** There is no man who has power over the spirit to contain the spirit; neither does he have power over the day of death. There is no discharge in war; neither shall wickedness deliver those who practice it.

9 All this I have seen, and applied my mind to every work that is done under the sun. There is a time in which one man has power over another to his hurt. **10** So I saw the wicked buried. Indeed they came also from holiness. They went and were forgotten in the city where they did this. This also is vanity. **11** Because sentence against an evil work is not executed speedily, therefore the heart of the sons of men is fully set in them to do evil. **12** Though a sinner commits crimes a hundred times, and lives long, yet surely I know that it will be better with those who fear God, who are reverent before him. **13** But it shall not be well with the wicked, neither shall he lengthen days like a shadow, because he doesn't fear God.

14 There is a vanity which is done on the earth, that there are righteous men to whom it happens according to the work of the wicked. Again, there are wicked men to whom it happens according to the work of the righteous. I said that this also is vanity.

15 Then I commended mirth, because a man has no better thing under the sun than to eat, to drink, and to be joyful: for that will accompany him in his labor all the days of his life which God has given him under the sun.

16 When I applied my heart to know wisdom, and to see the business that is done on the earth (even though eyes see no sleep day or night), **17** then I saw all the work of God, that man can't find out the work that is done under the sun, because however much a man labors to seek it out, yet he won't find it. Yes even though a wise man thinks he can comprehend it, he won't be able to find it.

OBSERVATION:
What do you notice? Write your questions.

WHO? Who speaks or is spoken to? Who is present or mentioned?

_____
_____
_____
_____
_____

WHAT? What action or dialogue has taken place? What questions does this bring up?

_____
_____
_____
_____
_____
_____
_____

WHERE? Whose house? What city? What nation?

_____
_____
_____
_____
_____

WHEN? What time, what day, what week, after what, etc?

_____
_____
_____
_____
_____

WHY? What led to the action or dialogue that took place in this passage? Record every question you have about the purpose for what is said or done.

_____
_____
_____
_____
_____
_____
_____
_____
_____
_____
_____
_____

OTHER QUESTIONS & OBSERVATIONS

_____
_____
_____
_____
_____
_____
_____
_____
_____
_____
_____
_____
_____
_____

CONTENT Record figures of speech, questions and answers, lists, comparisons, etc. What questions do these bring up?

_____
_____
_____
_____
_____
_____
_____
_____
_____

CONTEXT What is the immediate context and the broader context? What happens right before and after this passage?

_____
_____
_____
_____
_____
_____

COMPARISON Track down scripture quotations, compare similar passages, notice other uses in scripture of special terms, names, or ideas.

_____
_____
_____
_____
_____
_____
_____

CULTURE How does the cultural context influence this passage? What questions do you need answered about the culture to understand it better?

_____
_____
_____
_____
_____
_____
_____
_____
_____

CONSULTATION Explore commentaries and sermons on this passage and record helpful thoughts.

_____
_____
_____
_____
_____
_____
_____
_____
_____
_____
_____
_____
_____
_____

APPLICATION
Keeping in mind the meaning of this passage in its original context, how can you apply this passage to your life?

_____
_____
_____
_____
_____
_____
_____
_____
_____
_____
_____
_____
_____
_____
_____
_____
_____
_____
_____
_____
_____
_____
_____
_____
_____
_____
_____

9 For all this I laid to my heart, even to explore all this: that the righteous, and the wise, and their works, are in the hand of God; whether it is love or hatred, man doesn't know it; all is before them. **²** All things come alike to all. There is one event to the righteous and to the wicked; to the good, to the clean, to the unclean, to him who sacrifices, and to him who doesn't sacrifice. As is the good, so is the sinner; he who takes an oath, as he who fears an oath. **³** This is an evil in all that is done under the sun, that there is one event to all: yes also, the heart of the sons of men is full of evil, and madness is in their heart while they live, and after that they go to the dead. **⁴** For to him who is joined with all the living there is hope; for a living dog is better than a dead lion. **⁵** For the living know that they will die, but the dead don't know anything, neither do they have any more a reward; for their memory is forgotten. **⁶** Also their love, their hatred, and their envy has perished long ago; neither do they any longer have a portion forever in anything that is done under the sun.

⁷ Go your way—eat your bread with joy, and drink your wine with a merry heart; for God has already accepted your works. **⁸** Let your garments be always white, and don't let your head lack oil. **⁹** Live joyfully with the wife whom you love all the days of your life of vanity, which he has given you under the sun, all your days of vanity, for that is your portion in life, and in your labor in which you labor under the sun. **¹⁰** Whatever your hand finds to do, do it with your might; for there is no work, nor plan, nor knowledge, nor wisdom, in Sheol, where you are going.

¹¹ I returned and saw under the sun that the race is not to the swift, nor the battle to the strong, neither yet bread to the wise, nor yet riches to men of understanding, nor yet favor to men of skill; but time and chance happen to them all.

[12] For man also doesn't know his time. As the fish that are taken in an evil net, and as the birds that are caught in the snare, even so are the sons of men snared in an evil time, when it falls suddenly on them.

[13] I have also seen wisdom under the sun in this way, and it seemed great to me. [14] There was a little city, and few men within it; and a great king came against it, besieged it, and built great bulwarks against it. [15] Now a poor wise man was found in it, and he by his wisdom delivered the city; yet no man remembered that same poor man. [16] Then I said, "Wisdom is better than strength." Nevertheless the poor man's wisdom is despised, and his words are not heard. [17] The words of the wise heard in quiet are better than the cry of him who rules among fools. [18] Wisdom is better than weapons of war; but one sinner destroys much good.

OBSERVATION:
What do you notice? Write your questions.

WHO? Who speaks or is spoken to? Who is present or mentioned?

_____
_____
_____
_____
_____
_____

WHAT? What action or dialogue has taken place? What questions does this bring up?

_____
_____
_____
_____
_____
_____
_____
_____
_____

WHERE? Whose house? What city? What nation?

_____
_____
_____
_____
_____
_____

WHEN? What time, what day, what week, after what, etc?

_____
_____
_____
_____
_____
_____

WHY? What led to the action or dialogue that took place in this passage? Record every question you have about the purpose for what is said or done.

_____
_____
_____
_____
_____
_____
_____
_____
_____
_____

OTHER QUESTIONS & OBSERVATIONS

_____
_____
_____
_____
_____
_____
_____
_____
_____
_____
_____
_____
_____
_____
_____

CONTENT Record figures of speech, questions and answers, lists, comparisons, etc. What questions do these bring up?

_____
_____
_____
_____
_____
_____
_____
_____
_____
_____

CONTEXT What is the immediate context and the broader context? What happens right before and after this passage?

_____
_____
_____
_____
_____
_____

COMPARISON Track down scripture quotations, compare similar passages, notice other uses in scripture of special terms, names, or ideas.

_____
_____
_____
_____
_____
_____
_____

CULTURE How does the cultural context influence this passage? What questions do you need answered about the culture to understand it better?

_____
_____
_____
_____
_____
_____
_____
_____

CONSULTATION Explore commentaries and sermons on this passage and record helpful thoughts.

_____
_____
_____
_____
_____
_____
_____
_____
_____
_____
_____
_____
_____
_____

APPLICATION
Keeping in mind the meaning of this passage in its original context, how can you apply this passage to your life?

_____
_____
_____
_____
_____
_____
_____
_____
_____
_____
_____
_____
_____
_____
_____
_____
_____
_____
_____
_____
_____
_____
_____
_____

10 Dead flies cause the oil of the perfumer to produce an evil odor; so does a little folly outweigh wisdom and honor.
² A wise man's heart is at his right hand,
but a fool's heart at his left. ³ Yes also when the fool walks by the way, his understanding fails him, and he says to everyone that he is a fool. ⁴ If the spirit of the ruler rises up against you, don't leave your place; for gentleness lays great offenses to rest. ⁵ There is an evil which I have seen under the sun, the sort of error which proceeds from the ruler. ⁶ Folly is set in great dignity, and the rich sit in a low place. ⁷ I have seen servants on horses, and princes walking like servants on the earth. ⁸ He who digs a pit may fall into it; and whoever breaks through a wall may be bitten by a snake. ⁹ Whoever carves out stones may be injured by them. Whoever splits wood may be endangered by it. ¹⁰ If the ax is blunt, and one doesn't sharpen the edge, then he must use more strength; but skill brings success.
¹¹ If the snake bites before it is charmed, then is there no profit for the charmer's tongue. ¹² The words of a wise man's mouth are gracious; but a fool is swallowed by his own lips. ¹³ The beginning of the words of his mouth is foolishness; and the end of his talk is mischievous madness. ¹⁴ A fool also multiplies words.

Man doesn't know what will be; and that which will be after him, who can tell him? ¹⁵ The labor of fools wearies every one of them; for he doesn't know how to go to the city.
¹⁶ Woe to you, land, when your king is a child,
    and your princes eat in the morning!

17 Happy are you, land, when your king is the son of nobles,
and your princes eat in due season,
for strength, and not for drunkenness!
18 By slothfulness the roof sinks in;
and through idleness of the hands the house leaks.
19 A feast is made for laughter,
and wine makes the life glad;
and money is the answer for all things.
20 Don't curse the king, no, not in your thoughts;
and don't curse the rich in your bedroom:
for a bird of the sky may carry your voice,
and that which has wings may tell the matter.

OBSERVATION:
What do you notice? Write your questions.

WHO? Who speaks or is spoken to? Who is present or mentioned?

_____
_____
_____
_____
_____
_____

WHAT? What action or dialogue has taken place? What questions does this bring up?

_____
_____
_____
_____
_____
_____
_____

WHERE? Whose house? What city? What nation?

_____
_____
_____
_____
_____

WHEN? What time, what day, what week, after what, etc?

_____
_____
_____
_____
_____

WHY? What led to the action or dialogue that took place in this passage? Record every question you have about the purpose for what is said or done.

OTHER QUESTIONS & OBSERVATIONS

CONTENT Record figures of speech, questions and answers, lists, comparisons, etc. What questions do these bring up?

_____
_____
_____
_____
_____
_____
_____
_____
_____
_____

CONTEXT What is the immediate context and the broader context? What happens right before and after this passage?

_____
_____
_____
_____
_____
_____
_____

COMPARISON Track down scripture quotations, compare similar passages, notice other uses in scripture of special terms, names, or ideas.

_____
_____
_____
_____
_____
_____
_____
_____

CULTURE How does the cultural context influence this passage? What questions do you need answered about the culture to understand it better?

_____
_____
_____
_____
_____
_____
_____
_____
_____

CONSULTATION Explore commentaries and sermons on this passage and record helpful thoughts.

_____
_____
_____
_____
_____
_____
_____
_____
_____
_____
_____
_____

APPLICATION
Keeping in mind the meaning of this passage in its original context, how can you apply this passage to your life?

_____
_____
_____
_____
_____
_____
_____
_____
_____
_____
_____
_____
_____
_____
_____
_____
_____
_____
_____
_____
_____
_____
_____
_____
_____
_____
_____
_____
_____

11 Cast your bread on the waters;

  for you shall find it after many days.

2 Give a portion to seven, yes, even to eight;

  for you don't know what evil will be on the earth.

3 If the clouds are full of rain, they empty themselves on the earth;

  and if a tree falls toward the south, or toward the north,

  in the place where the tree falls, there shall it be.

4 He who observes the wind won't sow;

  and he who regards the clouds won't reap.

5 As you don't know what is the way of the wind,

  nor how the bones grow in the womb of her who is with child;

  even so you don't know the work of God who does all.

6 In the morning sow your seed,

  and in the evening don't withhold your hand;

  for you don't know which will prosper, whether this or that,

  or whether they both will be equally good.

7 Truly the light is sweet,

  and it is a pleasant thing for the eyes to see the sun.

8 Yes, if a man lives many years, let him rejoice in them all;

  but let him remember the days of darkness, for they shall be many.

  All that comes is vanity.

9 Rejoice, young man, in your youth,

  and let your heart cheer you in the days of your youth,

  and walk in the ways of your heart,

  and in the sight of your eyes;

  but know that for all these things God will bring you into judgment.

10 Therefore remove sorrow from your heart,
   and put away evil from your flesh;
   for youth and the dawn of life are vanity.

OBSERVATION:

What do you notice? Write your questions.

WHO?
Who speaks or is spoken to? Who is present or mentioned?

_____

_____

_____

_____

_____

WHAT?
What action or dialogue has taken place? What questions does this bring up?

_____

_____

_____

_____

_____

_____

_____

WHERE?
Whose house? What city? What nation?

_____

_____

_____

_____

_____

WHEN?
What time, what day, what week, after what, etc?

_____

_____

_____

_____

_____

WHY? What led to the action or dialogue that took place in this passage? Record every question you have about the purpose for what is said or done.

_____
_____
_____
_____
_____
_____
_____
_____
_____
_____
_____
_____

OTHER QUESTIONS & OBSERVATIONS

_____
_____
_____
_____
_____
_____
_____
_____
_____
_____
_____
_____
_____
_____
_____
_____

CONTENT Record figures of speech, questions and answers, lists, comparisons, etc. What questions do these bring up?

_____
_____
_____
_____
_____
_____
_____
_____
_____
_____

CONTEXT What is the immediate context and the broader context? What happens right before and after this passage?

_____
_____
_____
_____
_____
_____

COMPARISON Track down scripture quotations, compare similar passages, notice other uses in scripture of special terms, names, or ideas.

_____
_____
_____
_____
_____
_____

CULTURE How does the cultural context influence this passage? What questions do you need answered about the culture to understand it better?

_____
_____
_____
_____
_____
_____
_____
_____
_____

CONSULTATION Explore commentaries and sermons on this passage and record helpful thoughts.

_____
_____
_____
_____
_____
_____
_____
_____
_____
_____
_____
_____
_____
_____
_____

APPLICATION
Keeping in mind the meaning of this passage in its original context, how can you apply this passage to your life?

_____
_____
_____
_____
_____
_____
_____
_____
_____
_____
_____
_____
_____
_____
_____
_____
_____
_____
_____
_____
_____
_____
_____
_____
_____
_____
_____
_____
_____
_____

12 Remember also your Creator in the days of your youth,
before the evil days come, and the years draw near,
when you will say, "I have no pleasure in them;"
² Before the sun, the light, the moon, and the stars are darkened,
and the clouds return after the rain;
³ in the day when the keepers of the house shall tremble,
and the strong men shall bow themselves,
and the grinders cease because they are few,
and those who look out of the windows are darkened,
⁴ and the doors shall be shut in the street;
when the sound of the grinding is low,
and one shall rise up at the voice of a bird,
and all the daughters of music shall be brought low;
⁵ yes, they shall be afraid of heights,
and terrors will be on the way;
and the almond tree shall blossom,
and the grasshopper shall be a burden,
and desire shall fail;
because man goes to his everlasting home,
and the mourners go about the streets:
⁶ before the silver cord is severed,
or the golden bowl is broken,
or the pitcher is broken at the spring,
or the wheel broken at the cistern,
⁷ and the dust returns to the earth as it was,
and the spirit returns to God who gave it.
⁸ "Vanity of vanities," says the Preacher.
"All is vanity!"

9 Further, because the Preacher was wise, he still taught the people knowledge. Yes, he pondered, sought out, and set in order many proverbs. **10** The Preacher sought to find out acceptable words, and that which was written blamelessly, words of truth. **11** The words of the wise are like goads; and like nails well fastened are words from the masters of assemblies, which are given from one shepherd. **12** Furthermore, my son, be admonished: of making many books there is no end; and much study is a weariness of the flesh.

13 This is the end of the matter. All has been heard. Fear God and keep his commandments; for this is the whole duty of man. **14** For God will bring every work into judgment, with every hidden thing, whether it is good, or whether it is evil.

OBSERVATION:
What do you notice? Write your questions.

WHO? Who speaks or is spoken to? Who is present or mentioned?

_____
_____
_____
_____
_____
_____

WHAT? What action or dialogue has taken place? What questions does this bring up?

_____
_____
_____
_____
_____
_____
_____
_____

WHERE? Whose house? What city? What nation?

_____
_____
_____
_____
_____
_____
_____

WHEN? What time, what day, what week, after what, etc?

_____
_____
_____
_____
_____
_____
_____

WHY? What led to the action or dialogue that took place in this passage?
Record every question you have about the purpose for what is said or done.

_____
_____
_____
_____
_____
_____
_____
_____
_____
_____

OTHER QUESTIONS & OBSERVATIONS

_____
_____
_____
_____
_____
_____
_____
_____
_____
_____
_____
_____
_____
_____

CONTENT
Record figures of speech, questions and answers, lists, comparisons, etc. What questions do these bring up?

_____
_____
_____
_____
_____
_____
_____
_____
_____

CONTEXT
What is the immediate context and the broader context? What happens right before and after this passage?

_____
_____
_____
_____
_____
_____

COMPARISON
Track down scripture quotations, compare similar passages, notice other uses in scripture of special terms, names, or ideas.

_____
_____
_____
_____
_____
_____

CULTURE
How does the cultural context influence this passage? What questions do you need answered about the culture to understand it better?

_____
_____
_____
_____
_____
_____
_____
_____
_____

CONSULTATION
Explore commentaries and sermons on this passage and record helpful thoughts.

_____
_____
_____
_____
_____
_____
_____
_____
_____
_____
_____
_____
_____
_____

APPLICATION
Keeping in mind the meaning of this passage in its original context, how can you apply this passage to your life?

_____
_____
_____
_____
_____
_____
_____
_____
_____
_____
_____
_____
_____
_____
_____
_____
_____
_____
_____
_____
_____
_____
_____
_____
_____

Ready for more bible study?

Find inductive bible study workbooks for every book of the bible:

www.biblestudyworkbooks.com

Scan the QR code to be taken directly to the full collection of inductive bible study workbooks!

Grab yours now!

Did you enjoy this workbook?

If you enjoyed this workbook and found it helpful, please leave a starred review on the Amazon listing! Reviews help more people like you find the book and start studying God's word on a deeper level.

Overall rating

☆☆☆☆☆

Add a headline

What's most important to know?

Add a photo or video

Shoppers find images and videos more helpful than text alone.

+

Add a written review

What did you like or dislike? What did you use this product for?

We will notify you via email as soon as your review is processed.

Submit

Thank you!

Made in the USA
Columbia, SC
06 January 2025

51207666R00054